Class 20s in colour

Photographs from the 1960s to the present day

Andrew Fell

ISBN 1 85780 020 6

Published in 1994 by
Midland Publishing Limited
24 The Hollow, Earl Shilton
Leicester, LE9 7NA, England.
Tel: 0455 847 256

Printed in Hong Kong
via World Print Limited.

Designed by
Stephen Thompson Associates
and Midland Publishing Limited.

Enthusiasts interested in helping
with the preservation of
examples of the class should
contact the Class 20 Locomotive Society by writing to:
David Beecham,
c/o 58 Strafford Gate,
Potters Bar, Hertfordshire
EN6 1PN.

Above: On Wednesday 4th June 1986, a Class 45 on a Liverpool to
Newcastle train overtakes a pair of Class 20s on a north-bound freight
at Copmanthorpe, just south of York. The 45's have long been
withdrawn but the Class 20s have soldiered on into the 1990s.
Tom Ferris, Pentax MG, Tokina 35-200mm, Kodachrome 64, f5.6.

Front cover photograph:

The combination of ex-works
Merry-Go-Round wagons,
semaphores, and a glorious blue
sky, make for a very striking
picture of 20 052 and 004 as
they approach Worksop station
with an east-bound MGR train
from Manton Colliery on 6th
September 1989. 20 052 was
withdrawn just over a year after
this photograph was taken,
being condemned on 17th
November 1990, whilst 20 004,
one of the first members of the
class dating from 1957, had
been withdrawn a month earlier
on 11th October 1990.

Les Nixon,
Pentax 6x7, 150mm Takumar,
Fujichrome 100, 1/500, f6.3.

Title page photograph:

The Leicester-Peterborough line
was closed every Sunday for
essential engineering work
during the autumn/winter of
1991. As a result, the Midland
main line between Syston
Junction and Toton saw a large
number of engineers' trains
conveying ballast, spoil and
track to and from the site of the
work. This train could be heard
some miles off as it approached
Syston Junction and turned
north onto the main line. At
08.18 in the morning, 20 142
and 215 pass Cossington on the
6th October 1991.

Andrew Fell, Pentax Spotmatic,
135mm Carl Zeiss,
Fujichrome 100, 1/250, f5.6.

Author's note

I am greatly indebted to the
photographers' whose work is
featured in this album. Their
foresight in recording the Class
20s in the years when they were
commonplace can only now be
appreciated. I am particularly
grateful to Pip Dunn, historical
consultant to the Class 20
Locomotive Society, for his help
and advice in producing this
book. I would also like to record
my thanks to Philip Sutton and
to members of the staff of *Rail*
magazine for their help in
various ways.

Andrew Fell, May 1994.

Back cover photograph:

Two of the last vacuum-braked-
only Class 20s, 20 077 and 141
emerge from Dove Holes Tunnel
on 30th May 1984 with an
empty limestone train returning
from ICI Winnington, near
Northwich, to Tunstead Quarry.
Both machines received dual
brakes at Derby works in 1986,
when they were repainted into
'Railfreight' livery. The
conversion was short-lived for
20 077 however, as it was
written off at Bickershaw
Colliery in April 1988. Parts
from the withdrawn locomotive
were donated to 20 088.

Les Nixon, Pentax 6x7,
105mm Takumar,
Ektachrome EPN, 1/250, f8.

Class 20　　　　Fact File

Type	English Electric Type 1
Class codes	D10/3, later 10/3, later 20
Introduced	1957 - 1968
Wheel arrangement	Bo-Bo
Production	**Batch 1**
Original number range	D8000 - D8049
TOPS number range **	20 050, 20 001 to 20 049
TOPS design codes	20-0aV / 20-0bX*
Weight (tonnes)	73.9 / 73.5*
Route indicator equipment	Disc
	Batch 2
Original number range	D8050 - D8127
TOPS number range	20 128, 20 051 to 20 127
TOPS design codes	20-0cV / 20-0dX*
Weight (tonnes)	73.0 / 73.4*
Route indicator equipment	Disc
	Batch 3
Original number range	D8128 - D8199, D8300 - D8327
TOPS number range	20 228, 20 129 to 20 227

TOPS design codes	20-0eV/20-0fX*
Weight (tonnes)	73.2 / 73.5*
Route indicator equipment	4-character headcode box
Manufacturers	English Electric Vulcan Foundry
	D8000 - D8019, D8035 - D8049 D8128 - D8327
	Robert Stephenson & Hawthorn
	D8020 - D8034, D8050 - D8127
Length	46ft 9½ in (14.25 m)
Width	8ft 9 in (2.67 m)
Height	12ft 7⅝ in (3.86 m)
Brake force	35 tonnes
Maximum speed	75 mph (rev'd May 1987 to 60 mph)
Route availability	6 for D8000 - D8019 until 1969; thereafter 5 for whole class
Train heating	None
Multiple working code	Blue star

Brake type	Vacuum, then dual
Sanding equipment	Pneumatic
Diesel engine type	English Electric 8 cylinder, 4 stroke 8SVT Mk II
Power	1000 hp (746kW) at 850 rpm available between 5 mph and maximum speed
Power at rail	770 hp (574kW)
Tractive effort (Max)	42,000 lb (187kN)
(Continuous)	25,000 lb (111kN) at 11 mph
Cylinder bore	10in
Cylinder stroke	12in
Cooling water capacity	130 gal
Lub oil capacity	100 gal
Fuel tank size	380 gal (1040 gal, 20 084 only)
Main generator type	EE 819 / 8C
Auxiliary generator	EE 991 / 2B
Power control equipment	4 x English Electric axle-hung traction motors.

Power control equipment (contd)	Type EE 526 / 5D (20 001 - 20 050) Type EE 526 / 8D (20 051 - 20 228)
Gear ratio	63 : 17
Wheel diameter	3ft 7in (1.092m)
Wheelbase	32ft 6in (9.91m)
Bogie wheel base	8ft 6in (2.59m)
Bogie pivot centres	24ft (7.315m)
Minimum curve negotiable	3½ chains (70.41m)

(* indicates examples converted to dual brakes)
(** TOPS = Total Operations Processing System)

Suggested further reading

English Electric Little Wonders:
Colin Marsden; Railway Magazine
November 1991 issue, pp 764 / 772.

British Rail Main Line Diesel Locomotives:
Colin J Marsden and Graham B Fenn;
Oxford Publishing Company, 1988.

20 221 was delivered to the Scottish Region in December 1967. Nearly 20 years later, on 4th July 1986, it was recorded at Kettlebridge on the Dundee to Edinburgh line, in charge of a featherweight freight. *Andrew Fell, Pentax Spotmatic, 50mm Takumar, Kodachrome 25, 1/500, f2.8.*

Introduction

The modernisation plan of the 1950's consisted of five different power ranges for the diesel locomotives to replace steam. The lowest power range was the Type A or Type 1, locomotives of 1000 hp or less. A variety of designs from a number of locomotive manufacturers were tried and it was English Electric's Type 1 that was allocated class code D10/3, later 10/3 and eventually Class 20, that became standard. This was a 73 tonne, single-cab locomotive, powered by the English Electric 8SVT Mk II diesel engine, with English Electric traction motors and generator equipment.

Twenty 'pilot scheme' locomotives were originally ordered. Allocated to Devons Road Depot, Bow, to work local freights in the London area, they also found service on some passenger turns. The class was a success from the very start, and orders for a further 108 locomotives followed, spreading the sphere of operation to the Scottish and Eastern Regions. Whilst the first twenty engines were built at the Vulcan Foundry, Newton-le-Willows, the later batches were split between the Vulcan Foundry and Robert Stephenson and Hawthorn Limited at Darlington. All 128 locomotives had been delivered by 1962. Later, when the other standard Type 1, the Class 17, had been deemed

unsatisfactory, a further 100 Class 20s were ordered and delivered between 1966 and 1968.

If the Class 20's good point was its simple well-proven design, its single cab was to be its greatest handicap; the limitations of the type's visibility dictated that Class 20s operating nose first should have two drivers as it was not deemed possible that one driver could have an adequate view of the road ahead. However, double-heading with the cabs outer-most eliminated this problem. Changing traffic requirements saw the pick-up freight disappearing in favour of the more economical block trains and generally heavier freights that required more than 1000 hp at the head. Hence the operation of the Class 20s in pairs became very much the norm.

The Class 20s were well established on the Scottish, Eastern and London Midland Regions of British Rail. They made infrequent visits to the Western Region, and very occasional sorties onto the Southern. The concentration of their freight work in the north of the country tended to restrict the class to those areas.

The absence of train-heating on Class 20s meant that for much of the year, passenger use was highly undesirable and thus only occurred on a very

sporadic and 'as necessary' basis. BR's deployment of Class 20s on passenger turns, most notably to Skegness, was entered into more by mistake than deliberate intention. They also worked to other seaside resorts on occasion and in the later years Llandudno was also a frequent destination. However, the coverage these Class 20 workings received in the railway press distorts the fact that passenger diagrams were few and far between.

The fitting of dual brakes commenced in 1967 and by 1976 about a quarter of the class had been equipped. Uncertainty about the future, due to a downturn in traffic, saw this programme halted until 1982 when it recommenced, and by 1986 all Class 20s remaining in traffic had been so equipped. Many Class 20s had also been fitted with slow speed control, reflecting the replacement of vacuum-braked coal trains by 'Merry-Go-Round' workings. The Class 20s seemed to have a place in BR's future freight requirements, but 1986 saw Railfreight move towards type 5 motive power instead of the lower powered engines and the plan to eliminate Class 20s through the introduction of the Class 60s became a reality. In March 1987, 20 154 became the last Class 20 to receive an overhaul and withdrawals accelerated. By

the beginning of 1994 just twenty-eight locomotives remained in service of which eighteen were in store.

Testimony to the successful design of the Class 20s is the fact that so many have exchanged their BR careers for a new lease of life under private ownership. In 1989, Hunslet-Barclay Limited bought seven Class 20s to convert to sub-class 20/9 standard, for use on weed killing duties over the length and breadth of the country. Six were converted with the seventh being used for spares. RFS Industries at Doncaster then bought fifteen Class 20s for use on track-laying duties for the Channel Tunnel project. The 20s were chosen in preference to German Class 211 locomotives which they out-performed in terms of power and exhaust emissions: a critical factor within the confines of the tunnel. Another four Class 20s were bought by Chemins de Fer Departmentaux, for use in France. In addition, a number of locomotives have been obtained for use on telecommunications trains and railway enthusiasts have secured the preservation of several members of the class; thus ensuring that these well loved and long lived workhorses will still be around for many years to come.

Andrew Fell,
May 1994.

4

D8035 and train is occupying the up fast line while excavators load chalk into the wagons. General Post Office mail pick up apparatus is visible on the right of the photograph as well as a hut where the mail pouches are stored. D8305 was just eight months old when this photograph was taken, having entered traffic in September 1959. Although initially allocated to Norwich depot, this was on paper only, as D8035 and several of her sisters actually went to Willesden in the same month they were delivered. At the time of writing the engine is still operating, as a Chemins de Fer Departmentaux locomotive in France.

Colour-Rail.

Less than two years into its career, Willesden-based D8036 is operating wrong line on the up-fast with an engineering train, with what appears to be another engine on the other end. The engine has yet to receive yellow warning panels of any description. 20 036, as this locomotive became, was withdrawn in June 1984 as a result of a collision, and was disposed of at BREL Glasgow two years later, having donated some parts to return 20 020 to traffic.

Colour-Rail,
Kodachrome II, 1/60 f11.

D8029 waits in the bay at Elgin with a train for the former Great North of Scotland branch to Lossiemouth on 5th June 1963. D8029 was one of a trio of locomotives which entered service in December 1959 at Leith Central shed in Edinburgh. As 20 029 the machine lasted until July 1991 when it was withdrawn from service at Thornaby.

Colour-Rail.

On 6th May 1965 D8033 propels a crew training special, made up of a single railcar, through Rotherham. D8033 was one of a batch subcontracted by English Electric to Robert Stephenson & Hawthorn Limited and built at their works in Darlington.

D8033 entered service in February 1960 at Inverness. Tinsley was the final depot for 20 033. It was withdrawn in November 1987 and cut up shortly afterwards at Crewe.

Geoff Warnes / Colour-Rail.

D8095 skirts the shores of Loch Trieg, some 15 miles east of Fort William with a down pick-up goods, a type of working on which the Class 20s were employed for so many years. D8095, later 20 095, was a Scottish Region locomotive up until 1978 when it went south of the border, before returning to Scotland in May 1984. The locomotive ended its days at Thornaby having also had spells at Tinsley, Immingham and Toton in the course of its career.

Michael Mensing,
Nikkorex 'F', 50mm Nikkor,
Agfacolour CT18, 1/500, f3.2.

The engines numbered D8070 to D8127 were all allocated to Scotland. The last of these heads a northbound freight at Polquhap on the former Glasgow & South Western main line in the summer of 1965. The locomotive has been given small yellow warning panels and was the last machine to be built with the disc-type train identification equipment. Locomotives from D8128 onwards were constructed at the Vulcan foundry, fitted with the 4-position route indicator boxes. D8127 was delivered new to Polmadie in July 1962. It was the last of the class to be built by Robert Stephenson & Hawthorn and marked the end of the first phase of the type's construction. The first locomotive of the next batch was not delivered until January 1966.

Colour-Rail.

D8112 passes Jordan Hill on the electrified Glasgow-Helensburgh route on 24th September 1965. This mixed freight is headed by three Mk1 coaches and a number of 'presflo' wagons are also in the formation. D8112 belonged to the second batch to be delivered to Scotland. The lion's share of these locomotives went to Eastfield depot including this one. The tablet-catching apparatus recess is apparent on this locomotive although some members of the class never actually had the equipment fitted. The larger cabside windows given to these locomotives were reputedly to aid drivers whilst leaning out of the cab to exchange tokens.

I P V Jones / Colour-Rail, Agfa CT18.

D8148 is seen here on a north bound test-train in the Lune Gorge,on the West Coast main line. The date is 16th June 1966 and according to the records, the locomotive was accepted into traffic at Toton on 2nd July of that year. The 'T' in the headcode signifies a test-train from Edge Hill, Liverpool, bound for Penrith. The stock consists mainly of ex-LMS coaches, probably condemned judging by the evidence of broken windows. These workings were used to test locomotives newly released from the Vulcan Foundry.

Bryan Hicks, Baldamatic 1, Agfa CT18, 1/500, f4.

The following three delightful pictures, taken on a sunny summer day in 1966 on the beautiful Speyside line in Scotland, provide a reminder of not just the sort of work the Class were called upon to do in those days, but of the pick-up freight, a relic of the age of steam, no longer to be seen on the railways of Britain. D8032 arrives at Craigellachie with its short train of wagons and a brake van which formed the 10.10 working from Aviemore.

Colour-Rail.

The return working on that day, 29th June 1966, was photographed beside the River Spey near Craigellachie.The train, the 14.00 from Craigellachie to Aviemore, collected traffic from various distilleries along the route. D8032 was only six years old when this photograph was taken. The locomotive is fitted with snowploughs at both ends. This was a characteristic of the Scottish based engines as they were used single-headed on a regular basis. D8032 had not received the yellow warning panels by this date.

*Colour-Rail,
Kodachrome II, 1/250, f3.5.*

The pick-up freight from Craigellachie to Aviemore pauses at Dailuaine sidings near Carron. These sidings were shunted by a steam locomotive owned by the distillery they served. Part of this line between Aviemore and Boat of Garten, has been preserved, but the freight traffic from the Speyside distilleries, like countless other freight traffic flows, has long been abdicated to the roads.

Colour-Rail,
Kodachrome II.

D8125 is scarcely taxed by the two coach up local service which it is hauling at Bay of Nigg, just south of Aberdeen, in July 1966. The locomotives allocated to the Scottish Region had recesses below the cab side windows to make room for a single line tablet catcher should this equipment be required. This modification meant that the running number had to be squeezed onto the small space remaining below the cab window, as this picture shows.

Colour-Rail.

Another view of one of the trains used to test new locomotives on the West Coast main line. On 26th August 1966 D8152 passes through Tebay on such a working. The smoke rising from the steam shed in the background is a reminder that steam bankers were still in evidence over Shap at this time. D8152 entered service in August 1966 and was cut up at MC Processors, Glasgow, in November 1988.

Colour-Rail.

Toton allocated machines rest at their home depot. The locomotives are D8158, D8152 and D8151, which were one, two and three months old respectively when this picture was taken, on 2nd October 1966. D8158 and D8151 both ended their careers at Toton as 20 158 and 20 151.

D8152 later went to Scotland, being withdrawn from Haymarket as 20 152 in April 1988. Small yellow warning panels were being applied to new locomotives by this date.

Colour-Rail, Kodachrome II.

This delightful scene from the 1960s shows D8138 entering the original Birmingham Snow Hill station on 11th October 1966. The locomotive was just six months old at this time, having been allocated to London Midland Region, Birmingham Division in April of that year.

In late 1987 the renumbered 20 138 was fitted with radio electronic token block equipment (RETB) at Eastfield. In October 1991 it was one of the first two Class 20s to go to Cheriton for Channel Tunnel duties along with 20 087.

Michael Mensing,
Nikkorex 'F', 50mm Nikkor,
Agfacolor CT18, 1/250, f4.

19

This fascinating view, taken when steam was still operating on BR, shows corporate blue liveried D8308 hauling withdrawn steam locomotives at York Motive Power Depot. The first two steam engines are BR standard Class 3 2-6-0s, Nos 77002 and 77012. While at the rear is an ex-LNER 'B1', No 61123. The last fifty of the class were delivered in blue livery with full yellow ends, the livery the majority ended their lives in. D8308 was one of these, arriving at York depot in April 1967. Many of the Class 20s have had much longer lives than the BR standard steam locomotives which they helped to displace.

John Glover, Ilford Sportsman, Agfa CT18.

Pilot scheme locomotive D8011 stands outside the north end of Willesden Electric Depot on 7th October 1967. By this date the engine was nearly ten years old, having entered service in November 1957, yet the very last Class 20, D8327 was not delivered for another four months after this photograph was taken. In 1986, 20 011 as this engine became, had the distinction of reaching Penzance for refuelling in conjuction with a rail tour. The derailment of 37 196 at Truro prevented the entire train from reaching its destination.

John Glover,
Ilford Sportsman,
Agfa CT18.

21

D8307 shuffles a wagon round the yard at Malton on 16th August 1968. D8300-D8309 were the first ten locomotives of the final batch and were all allocated to York depot, D8307 entering service in April 1967. When the initial 20 machines were ordered as part of the pilot scheme for new locomotives under the 1955 Modernisation Plan, it was not envisaged that the type would be so successful that it would run to in excess of 200 locomotives. The number sequence from D82xx onwards was allocated to the BTH Type 1 diesels. Thus, when the additional 100 locomotives were ordered in the mid 1960s they had to take the numbers of the next available block and as a consequence the number sequence jumped from D8199 to D8300.

Colour-Rail.

This view shows D8033 in the departure line at Crewe Works on 26th January 1969. With the green livery still being applied as late as this plus a reputation for reliability that meant relatively infrequent visits to the works for overhaul, it is not surprising that some members of the class retained this livery until 1980. The tablet catching apparatus can be seen in some detail in this view. D8033 later became 20 033. It was withdrawn in November 1987 following collision damage, never having received dual-brakes.

John Glover,
Praktica Nova, f2.8 Tessar,
Agfa CT18.

The Class has had a long association with Toton Depot. D8168 was pictured there in May 1970 coupled to a type of vehicle which is now extinct, the brake tender. These vehicles had brakes on all eight wheels and were heavily ballasted. Diesel locomotives were not as heavy as the steam types they replaced and with heavy trains of unfitted goods wagons there was always the chance that the weight of the train could prove too much for the diesel at its head and push it out of control. By providing both increased brake power and by adding a considerable weight at the front, the brake tender was designed to overcome this disadvantage of the new motive power.

The late D H Beecroft / Colour-Rail.

20 060 stands in the paint-shop at Derby Works on 7th October 1973, in a half-finished state. The locomotive is réceiving the standard blue livery and was also renumbered at this time from D8060, following its overhaul at the works. In early 1989 this locomotive was renumbered for a second time when it became 20 902 *Lorna* and became part of the Hunslet-Barclay fleet of six locomotives.

Norman Preedy,
Pentax SPII, Agfa CT18.

This view of Gloucester Horton Road depot shows 20 173 stabled between duties on 22nd June 1975. The locomotive had worked an inter-regional freight from the London Midland Region, if the headcode is correct. The use of headcodes on BR was abandoned from January 1976. Gloucester was a regular Western Region location for Class 20s. Although they seldom ventured further south, some occasionally reached Bristol.

Norman Preedy,
Pentax SPII, Agfa CT18.

Toton thoroughbred 20 151 leads 20 167 on a coal train out of Rufford Colliery in the Nottinghamshire coalfield. A fine example of a Midland Railway lower quadrant semaphore overlooks the colliery entrance. The train would have taken a route along the ex-Midland Railway, Newark to Mansfield line, which was abandoned soon after this picture was taken. The destination of this train, recorded on 14th April 1977, was probably Ratcliffe Power Station.

Les Nixon,
Nikon F, 85 mm Nikkor,
Kodachrome 25.

20 151 and 20 030 are seen working, quite unusually, with both locomotives cab-first, at Ryecroft Junction, Walsall. This photograph was taken on the gloriously sunny evening of 21st June 1977. The leading locomotive is one of the last green survivors, although a replacement bodyside door is evident in blue livery.

Michael Mensing,
Bronica S2A, 75mm Nikkor,
Agfachrome 50s
(rated at 125 ASA), 1/500, f5.

20 030 and 050 haul a typical 1970s coal train past Whitacre on the Birmingham to Tamworth line. The black lining on 20 030's indicator discs was a trademark of Eastfield depot. This locomotive's moment of glory came in 1987 when it was named *River Rother* and painted in near original green livery. The trailing engine, 20 050, better known as D8000, had already been stored for a period of several months in 1975, and was withdrawn prematurely in 1980 to become part of the National Collection at York Railway Museum.

Michael Mensing,
Bronica S2A, 75mm Nikkor,
Agfachrome 50s
(rated at 125 ASA), 1/800, f5.6.

With red buffer beams and grey roofs still in evidence, if a little work-stained, a pair of green 20s, Nos 20 167 and 174 approach the Erewash Valley main line at Blackwell South Junction, as they leave Westhouses. Both these locomotives received dual brakes back in 1971. The pair left Toton for the first time in 1985 when they went to Tinsley as part of a large scale re-allocation of locomotives between the two depots. The signals, locomotives and wagons in this view are all history now.

Les Nixon, Leica M3, Kodachrome 25, 1/250, f4.

Green liveried 20 153 leads a rather tatty blue 20 068 at the head of a smart rake of Mk 1 stock on a Derby-Skegness train, past some superb semaphores guarding the eastern approach to Sleaford station on 19th August 1978. 20 153, despite its vintage appearance, was one of Toton's dual-braked Class 20s at this time. 20 068 was withdrawn in June 1987 whilst 20 153 was condemned in October 1987.

Les Nixon,
Leica M3, 90mm Elmarit,
Kodachrome 25, 1/250, f4.5.

This interesting photograph shows a green machine as late as 1979. 20 164 is paired with 20 158 on the 12.58 Skegness-Derby, seen at its destination on 16th June. 20 164 is immaculate, having only just come out of Crewe Works in May of that year. 20 158 is vacuum-braked only, making this an unusual pairing of vacuum and dual braked machines. Surprisingly, 20 158 has received the two spot headcode despite its outdated livery.

Norman Preedy,
Pentax SPII, Agfa CT18.

20 003 and 066 stand in Tinsley yard with train 9T34, a trip freight to Sheffield Freight Terminal, on 23rd September 1980. Alas, much of this traffic is now moved by road and the freight terminal itself is closed. 20 003, formerly D8003, like the other pilot scheme locomotives (D8000 to D8019) spent its initial years based in London and this particular example never received dual brakes due to its comparatively early withdrawal at the end of 1982. It was cut up at Crewe in 1984. 20 066 on the other hand, enjoyed an extra lease of life, being hired to work for RFS Industries at the Channel Tunnel site at Cheriton in Kent, between January 1992 and March 1993.

Paul Shannon,
Olympus OM1, 50mm lens,
Kodachrome 64, 1/250, f8-5.6.

This delightful mixed freight bought Class 20s to more unfamiliar territory on 2nd April 1982 as they head north up the East Coast main line, having just passed over Relly Mill Viaduct in County Durham. The locomotives in question are 20 044 and 006, both of which were stored at Toton in 1981, before being reinstated at Eastfield the following year. 20 006 was no stranger to Scotland, having been sent north of the border for a month in the Autumn of 1958 for trials. 20 044 had the distinction of ending its career on a passenger diagram. After working the 21.42 Crewe-Derby on 8th August 1989 it returned to Toton and was switched off for the last time.

Dorothy Robinson,
Pentax 6x7,
Ektachrome EPD, 1/500 f5.6.

Although pairs of 20s most often work coupled nose to nose, other combinations are not unknown, and Nos 20 101 and 028 make a welcome appearance with both engines working cab-first on a train of shale oil spoil to Carmyle (Glasgow), seen here at Hardengreen Junction, Edinburgh on 14th June 1982. 20 028 began its life in Scotland as D8028, part of the batch D8028 to D8034, originally fitted with tablet-catching apparatus, snow plough brackets and slightly larger cab-side windows. These modifications were subsequently also carried out on the engines numbered D8070 to D8127, which included the other locomotive seen here, 20 101 which was later renumbered 20 901.

Dorothy Robinson, Pentax 6x7, Ektachrome EPD, 1/500, f6.3.

In 1982, the absence of a large number of Class 37s due to damage following a particularly bad Scottish winter, led to a Class 20 working the Mallaig line on 22nd and 23rd of June. 20 191 had the honour and on the 22nd is seen at Mallaig awaiting departure with the 18.55 service to Fort William. The old style station nameboard has now sadly disappeared. 20 191, originally allocated to Toton, moved to Haymarket in March 1973, where it stayed for a decade, before returning to Toton in July 1983. In 1972, this locomotive along with D8179 (20 179) was fitted with slow speed control equipment for trials on coal trains in the Midlands. In 1985 it returned to Scotland for a second time on account of having this original type of slow speed control, BR wanting to concentrate loco-motives with this equipment on the Scottish Region. It returned south again in March 1987, this time to Bescot. Put in store two months later it was finally con-demned on 4th October 1987.

Peter J. Robinson,
Pentax 6x7, Ektachrome EPD,
1/125, f16-11.

20 114 poses at Fort William station on 21st July 1983, shunting the observation car used on the Mallaig line. From the late 1970s until March 1989 there was usually a Class 20 to be found acting as station pilot at Fort William. The 20 replaced an 08 shunter and undertook trip workings in the Fort William area. 20 114, as D8114, was delivered to Eastfield in February 1962 and apart from a spell at Toton between 1969 and 1973, remained a Scottish Region locomotive until March 1989, when it went back to Toton. 20 114 along with 20 127 and 138 was one of just three of the class to be fitted with radio electronic token block equipment (RETB) for use in the Scottish Highlands.

Tom Heavyside, Pentax Spotmatic, 55mm Takumar, Kodachrome 64, 1/250, f5.

The Class 20's earliest association with the Leicester to Skegness route was in 1973, when they deputised for a pair of Class 25s. In 1974 three pairs made the trip, again as substitute motive power, and although there were many more sightings the following year, it wasn't until 1976 that certain trains became diagrammed for Class 20 haulage. On 30th June 1984, 20 113 and 161 arrive at Loughborough, with the summer afternoon Skegness to Leicester service. 20 113 already devoid of indicator discs by this time, was to become an RFS locomotive, while 20 161, a Toton machine all its working life, was withdrawn in 1988 and cut up at Vic Berry's yard in Leicester in May 1990.

Gavin Morrison,
Pentax SP1000, 50mm lens,
Kodachrome 25, 1/250 f3.5.

Penmaenmawr Quarry   23rd July 1985

20 090 and 104 shunt at Penmaenmawr Quarry with ballast wagons from Springs Branch, Wigan on 23rd July 1985. This was probably the first visit of Railfreight liveried Class 20s to North Wales. At this time the class was still very rare at locations west of Point of Ayr Colliery. 20 104 was introduced to Eastfield in December 1961 and had only just been allocated south of the border, arriving at Toton in March 1985. 20 090 was also delivered new to Eastfield in September 1961. It was reallocated to Toton in November 1973, and apart from a period spent back in Scotland from May 1981 until March 1985, it remained a London Midland Region locomotive until condemned on 6th July 1993.

Larry Goddard, Olympus OM1, Zuiko 35-70mm zoom, Kodachrome 64, 1/250, f6.3.

An unusual combination of English Electric power is made even more striking because of the Class 20 working bonnet-first. 20 137 leads 37 102 as the duo power their way past Auchterauder on the Perth to Stirling line with a salt train on 14th July 1986. At the end of 1986 this Class 20 went to Derby Works and emerged in Railfreight livery, whereupon it was allocated to Thornaby. In June 1987 it was named *Murray B. Hofmeyr* thus bringing about a totally new identity for the former Scottish machine in the space of one year. Returning to Scotland in May 1990, it remained at Eastfield for just over a year before returning south, initially to Toton, though eventually to Thornaby.

Andrew Fell, Pentax Spotmatic, 50mm Takumar, Kodachrome 64, 1/1000, f2.8.

Autumn colours are very apparent in this cutting, near Kilsby, on the Rugby to Northampton line. The date is 23rd September 1986. The train depicted here is an additional freight for Northampton. The locomotives, 20 121 and 154 returned light engine later in the afternoon. Class 20s enjoyed a brief spell of activity in the Rugby area during the mid 1980s, although rapidly became scarce from 1986 onwards. The second locomotive, 20 154, was the last Class 20 to be overhauled, being released in March 1987, still in plain blue livery. This was because the Civil Engineering sector paid for the overhaul, and blue was still the official departmental livery at that time.

Andrew Fell, Pentax Spotmatic, 50mm Takumar, Kodachrome 25, 1/500, f2.8.

In 1986 eight Class 20s were modified with a triple valve braking system with a view to them being used exclusively on ICI stone trains in the Buxton area. The locomotives involved were renumbered and formed the 20/3 sub-class in April of that year. These machines were quickly ousted by Tinsley-based 37/5s, rendering the sub-class unnecessary. 20 305 and 306 were allocated to Thornaby before renumbering back to 20 172 and 20 173 respectively in November 1986, when they were also repainted and named. On 24th October, the pair were photographed shunting at Redmire Quarry with the Redcar limestone train.

Michael Rhodes, Canon AE-1, Kodachrome 64, 1/125, f5.6-4.

An immaculate 20 070, with red skirting, buffer beam and a white cab roof, hauls a lengthy freight, single-handed at Middlesborough on 13th December 1986. The train is a BSC Lackenby to Tees yard trip working. 20 070 was one of the first Class 20s to go to Thornaby in November 1986, whereupon it was immediately repainted in this smart colour scheme and given the name *Leyburn*.

Peter J. Robinson,
Pentax 6x7,
Ektachrome EPD, 1/500, f4.

Low winter sunshine catches the texture of drifted snow in this view taken on 28th January 1987. The rural location conveys the atmosphere of this now disused freight-only line, the Caldon Low Quarry branch in Staffordshire. The precise location of this photograph is Ipstone. 20 084 leads 20 020 on the climb to the summit from the quarry. The extra fuel tanks fitted to 20 084 are illustrated in this view. These were added at Crewe in 1985, and resulted in a three-fold increase in fuel capacity from 380 to 1040 gallons. 20 020, the first production series machine, is now preserved on the Bo'ness Railway in Scotland.

Les Nixon, Pentax 6x7, 105mm Takumar, Ektachrome 100, 1/250 f6.3.

A pair of pilot scheme Class 20s, 20 005 and 019, are seen heading south through Harbury cutting on the Leamington to Banbury line on 21st April 1987, with an engineers' train. The twenty pilot scheme locomotives were all built with oval buffers which some retained until the end of their careers, although much swapping of buffers took place over the years and engines sometimes had oval buffers at one end only. 20 005 was also delivered without handrails: the first seven engines didn't have these fitted originally. Both locomotives were delivered new to Devons Road Depot, Bow. D8005 arrived there in September 1957 and D8019 in March the following year.

Bryan Hicks,
Pentax MES,
Kodachrome 64, 1/500, f4.

One of the more far-flung places Class 20s visited on a diagrammed freight service was Aberystwyth. The train was the Wednesdays only oil working from Stanlow, and the return empties are seen here on 27th May 1987 behind 20 031 and 145. The location is Commins Coch, which lies between Machynlleth and Caersws. 20 031 is now preserved on the Keighley & Worth Valley Railway in Yorkshire. 20 145, which was the last 20 to carry the BR logo on the cabside, rather than bodyside position, has also enjoyed a reprieve. Initially sold to MC Metals for scrap, it was then bought by RFS and survived as 2019 in France. On 11th August 1993 it returned to England via the Channel Tunnel.

Les Nixon,
Pentax 6x7, 150mm Takumar
Ektachrome 100, 1/250, f6.3.

A well-photographed Class 20 rail-tour was that of 11th July 1987 when the *Stilton and Branston Ploughman* ran from Kings Cross to Paddington via Deepcar (Sheffield). 20 126 and 022 seen here, had replaced green-liveried machines 20 030 and 064. The train, resplendent with its maroon stock, is approaching Woodburn Junction, Sheffield, having come off the Nunnery branch and is seen here opposite the site of the new Super-Tram depot. 20 126 was a Scottish locomotive up until October 1986 when it came south to Tinsley. It was withdrawn in September 1989, just over a year after 20 022.

Les Nixon,
Pentax 6x7, 200mm Takumar Ektachrome 100.

Under a gloriously rich sky, 20 222 and 226 head the Oxwellmains to Craiginches cement train on the East Goods loop at Millerhill on the evening of 5th August 1987. 20 222 was a solid Scottish Region locomotive, starting life at Polmadie and ending it at Haymarket on 15th December 1987, following a traction motor fire. It was cut up at MC Metals, Glasgow the following year. Note the headlight fitted to this locomotive, unique to Scottish Region Class 20s, and also the larger size numbers on both engines.

Peter J. Robinson,
Pentax 6x7, Ektachrome EPD,
1/500, f5.6.

Coatham   24th November 1988

20 165 *Henry Pease* and
20 119 haul a potash train from
Boulby to Middlesborough on
24th November 1988. 20 119
along with sister engine 20 066
spent some time at work on the
Channel Tunnel site at Cheriton
near Folkestone. 20 119 was
replaced there by 20 132.

It was subsequently put in store
from June 1992 until it was
condemned on 25th September
1992.

Peter J. Robinson,
Pentax 6x7, Fujichrome 400,
1/500, f6.3.

49

Kettlebeck Bridge   11th March 1989

Diversions of steel trains over the Carnforth to Settle Junction line in March 1989 have been well documented, and no wonder if this view taken at Kettlebeck Bridge is typical of the scenery in the area. 20 075 and 023 head 6V39, the 7.30 Mossend-Margam steel train on 11th March – a rare appearance on a line that is normally devoid of loco-hauled trains. 20 023 had the distinction of being the first Class 20 to be painted in 'old style' Railfreight livery back in March 1985. It was fortunate enough to hold on to a full set of indicator discs, unlike 20 075 which had its discs removed after an overhaul at Crewe, emerging just four months earlier in December 1984, still in blue livery.

Gavin Morrison, Minolta 7000, zoom lens at 85mm, Kodachrome 64, 1/250, f5.6.

Two ex-Thornaby locomotives (with their very distinctive embellishments) haul 6M24, a Mossend to Dee Marsh steel train, diverted over the Carnforth to Settle Junction line on 11th March 1989. The locomotives, 20 028 and 172 carry the Thornaby kingfisher logo and 20 172 has extra large bodyside numbers, with the cabside numbers painted out – another Thornaby trademark.

Peter J. Robinson,
Pentax 6x7,
Fujichrome 400, 1/1000, f6.3.

The only Class 20 to make the transition into late 80s Railfreight livery was 20 088, although it never received sector markings or depot crests. The locomotive was repainted at Doncaster Works in 1988, being released back into traffic in July of that year. It is seen here at Stoke-on-Trent on 16th March 1989. This locomotive's career continued as RFS No 2017.

Hugh Ballantyne,
Leica M3, 90mm Summicron,
Kodachrome 25, 1/60, f5.6-4.

Although the exploits of the celebrity green machines have been well documented, it is interesting to see one on a more mundane duty, paired up with a typically dirty blue liveried sister locomotive. 20 098 leads 20 064 at Hasland on 10th May 1989. Chesterfield's famous crooked spire can be seen in the background. Both these locomotives were outbased at Frodingham, Scunthorpe at this time, and although 20 064 was actually a Civil Engineers sector locomotive, Frodingham was not too fussy about sector allocation, hence the sight of this duo on a steel train. 20 098 is now preserved on the Great Central Railway at Loughborough, whilst 20 064 was cut up in October 1991.

John S. Whiteley,
Pentax, 55mm lens,
Kodachrome 64, 1/500, f4.

Excellent visibility and a rich blue sea add to the merit of this highly scenic coastal view of a pair of Class 20s on the Boulby line. 20 118 and 165 are seen near Brotton on the steep gradient from Skinningrove on the 4th July 1989. Their train is yet another load of potash from the mine at Boulby. This pair was named together at Saltburn on 13th August 1987 and carried the names *Saltburn-by-the-Sea* (20 118) and *Henry Pease* (20 165). Both engines went to Eastfield in 1990.

David Rodgers,
Pentax MX, 50mm lens,
Kodachrome 25, 1/250, f3.8.

Ironbridge, 6th November 1989

Ratcliffe-on-Soar, 28th July 1989

Ironbridge was still a mecca for Class 20s in 1989. They had been an immediate success after replacing the Class 56s which had previously held sway on these duties. Seen here are 20 194 (with 20 016 out of view) and 20 080 and 135, progressing through the unloading stage, caught by low autumn sunshine on 6th November 1989. 20 135 was delivered new to Coventry in March 1966, but moved to Toton three and a half years later.

Courtesy of National Power plc, Ironbridge Power Station. Andrew Fell, Pentax Spotmatic, 50mm Takumar, Kodachrome 64, 1/125, f2.8.

With just one disc remaining, 20 052 leads 20 004 through the unloading stage at Ratcliffe-on-Soar power station on 28th July 1989. The powder-like nature of power station coal is evident, with large deposits on the grating below the rails. 20 004 entered service in August 1957 as D8004. It was withdrawn in 1990, after a career of more than 33 years. 20 052 entered service in March 1961 and was withdrawn a month after 20 004.

Courtesy of PowerGen plc. Ratcliffe-on-Soar Power Station.
Andrew Fell, Pentax Spotmatic, 50mm Takumar, Kodachrome 64, 1/15, f4.

Redhill Tunnel   17th August 1989

Viewed from above the portals of Redhill Tunnel, 20 186 and 103 draw out of Ratcliffe-on-Soar Power Station onto the down slow main line with MGR empties on the 17th August 1989.

Andrew Fell,
Mamiya 645J, 80mm Sekor,
Kodachrome 64, 1/250, F5.6-4.

Former Scottish Region engines 20 127 and 20 114 were two of the three Class 20s fitted with RETB for use in the Scottish Highlands, but by March 1989 this was superfluous as the locomotives were allocated away from Eastfield, down to Toton. These two 20s remained together as a pair through much of 1989 and on 24th September were caught in action on the trip working from Great Rocks Junction. 20 127, 110 and 102 each had a disc removed when a sealed beam headlight was fitted, creating the front end arrangement that can be seen here. This was much more discreet than the headlights fitted to the Class 45s.

*Andrew Fell,
Pentax Spotmatic,
50mm Takumar,
Kodachrome 64, 1/1000,
f4-2.8.*

In 1990 there were still four loco-hauled trains to Skegness on a summer Saturday but Class 20s were no longer diagrammed. However the class did appear on occasions, and Spring Bank Holiday Monday, 28th May witnessed 20 034 and 042 on the customary additional service from Derby. From 1988, when 20s were used on Skegness services, it was Toton departmental engines which were booked for these duties, and this pair exhibit the departmental stripes above the cabside numbers. The pair are enjoying a lengthy break at Skegness before setting off for Derby at 18.00 hours. Despite their numbers, 20 042 (D8042) entered service four months earlier than 20 034 (D8034).

Andrew Fell,
Mamiya 1000s, 80mm Sekor,
Ektachrome 100, 1/60, f22-16.

Seven Class 20s were bought by Hunslet-Barclay for use on the weed-killing trains which that firm operates. They were converted into a new sub-class, the 20/9s, at the Hunslet-Barclay works at Kilmarnock. Three pairs of locomotives were turned out for these duties, the seventh served as a source of spares to keep the others running. This magnificent view of Lockwood Viaduct at Huddersfield depicts 20 905 and 20 902 on a weed-killling train, traversing the Penistone line on 20th June 1990. 20 905, previously numbered 20 225 and D8325 before that, was built as a dual-braked machine, starting life at Polmadie in November 1967. This locomotive saw an unexpected return to revenue-earning traffic on 10th June 1992 when it was used to haul a failed 47 671 between Dalwhinnie and Blair Athol on the 10.15 Inverness-Edinburgh of that day.

John S Whiteley,
Nikon F301, 50mm lens,
Kodachrome 64, 1/500, f3.8.

In addition to their frequent excursions to Skegness, Class 20s started putting in regular appearances at another seaside resort, Llandudno. On 15th August 1991, 20 032 and 007 worked the 08.11 Derby-Llandudno, a loco-hauled train during the week, though worked by a DMU on Saturdays. The pair are passing a fine example of a North Staffordshire railway signalbox at Longport in the Potteries. This same pairing reached an even more distant seaside resort in 1992 when the duo visited Weymouth, on a railtour.

Hugh Ballantyne,
Leica M3, 50mm Summicron,
Kodachrome 25, 1/500, f2.8-2.

On a very windy autumnal afternoon, 5th November 1991, 20 128 and 168 put in an appearance on the Erewash Valley route at Langley Mill, with a southbound MGR train. Once a regular stamping ground for the class 20s, their appearances were rare by this date. 20 128 was numbered out of sequence, actually starting life as D8050 in March 1961 because the number 20 050 was allocated to the prototype D8000.

Andrew Fell,
Mamiya 1000s, 80mm Sekor,
Ektachrome 100, 1/500, f4.

RFS Class 20, formerly 20 084 (still to receive its new number of 2002) was recorded at Kilnhurst on 7th January 1992. After having asbestos removed at MC Metals, Glasgow, the RFS locomotives received the equivalent of a 'D' examination at Kilnhurst as well as a careful tuning to minimize exhaust emissions. A catalytic converter and silencer would be fitted in due course. 20 084 was the first engine to be painted in this, the colour scheme used by the CTTG (Channel Tunnel Trackwork Group) to whom the track laying work in the tunnel was sub-contracted. 20 084, along with 20 113, were the first two RFS Class 20s to be moved to the Channel Tunnel site where they joined their BR sisters 20 087, 138, 066 and 119. By 1994 these Class 20s had finished their duties at the Channel Tunnel construction sites and the allegedly financially troubled RFS were trying to sell them after plans to find alternative uses proved unsuccessful.

Philip Sutton, Nikon F4, 28-85mm AF Nikkor zoom, Fujichrome RDP100, 1/60, f5.6.

In marked contrast to her sisters which were hard at work at the Channel Tunnel site, the class leader was in genteel retirement as part of the National Railway Museum's collection. Alterations to the NRM at York, meant that locomotives had to be removed from the main hall, thus providing an opportunity to photograph these engines in daylight. D8000 alias 20 050, is seen here on 12th April 1992, prior to being positioned back in the main hall, shortly before the Museum's reopening. The English Electric 8SVT, 8 cylinder engine is clearly visible in this view of the locomotive with the bodyside doors removed.
20 050 was withdrawn on 14th December 1980 and repainted into original green livery in 1984.

Barry Nicolle,
Olympus OM1-MD, 50mm lens,
Fujichrome 100, 1/250, f11.

On Saturday and Sunday, the 25th and 26th of April 1992, Longsight depot in Manchester held open days to celebrate its 150th birthday. On the Saturday, Regional Railways (North West) organised a number of loco-hauled trains in conjuction with the event, using an impressive array of motive power. A pair of 20s operated a number of turns including the 12.48 Manchester-Barrow. 20 168 and 059 are seen here crossing the Lever Viaduct with this service. Both locomotives belonged to the Power Station Coal, North-West pool at this time.

Dean Cornthwaite,
Pentax SP1000,
50mm Takumar,
Kodachrome 64, 1/500 f5.6-4.

Ramsbottom **6th June 1992**

Preserved 20 031 departs from Ramsbottom with a Rawtenstall to Bury service on the occasion of a diesel weekend on the East Lancashire Railway. 20 031 is based on the Keighley & Worth Valley Railway in West Yorkshire, but had been hired out for the weekend. The K&WVR learnt that they had been successful in their bid for 20 031 on 7th June 1991. The engine carries standard rail blue livery with an Eastfield Scottish terrier logo and Immingham style orange lining. 20 031 was originally a Scottish locomotive, being delivered to Kittybrewster and also spending time at Inverness, but it left Scotland in 1968 and never returned.

Anthony Hicks,
Pentax ME Super,
Pentax 100mm lens,
Kodak Gold 200, 1/500, f8.

The 1990s have been exciting times for the many fans of the venerable Class 20s. They have appeared in several new liveries and been involved with what is surely the greatest railway development this century, the construction of the Channel Tunnel. Members of the class have even gone to work abroad for in 1992 the Compagnie de Chemins de Fer Departmentaux (CFD) acquired four Class 20s to work on its lines in France. The first of the quartet to cross the Channel was 20 139, which originally entered BR service in April 1966 as D8139. The

locomotive was shipped from Poole to Cherbourg and then went to Trappes depot in Paris for wheel turning. After extensive testing and evaluation the locomotive entered service on the CFD line from Autun to Avallon in November 1992. These pictures show the former 20 139 on the appraisal runs, at MontChanin, on 8th July 1992. Looking good in the striking CFD livery, it will be noted that the headcode boxes have been completely removed from both the front and back of the engine.

David Haycock.

67

A growing number of members of the class have been preserved privately. One of these, 20 227, put in an appearance at Bescot Open Day on 30th August 1992. The last Class 20 to be built, 20 227 was condemned on 16th September 1990 and the Class 20 Locomotive Society finally learnt that they had acquired the engine on 7th June 1991. It arrived at Swanwick on the Midland Railway Centre in September 1991 and made its debut on a passenger working there on the 12th of October in that year.

Philip Sutton,
Nikon F4,
28-85mm AF Nikkor zoom,
Fujichrome RDP100,
1/250, f8.

RFS Class 20s, Nos 2012 and 2020, are seen leaving the south running tunnel of the Channel Tunnel at Coquelles, France. They are hauling a track-laying train on 3rd November 1992. The huge exhaust fittings on the roofs of these engines pump fumes into 'scrubbers' so as to not pollute the working environment within the tunnel. 2012 began life as D8056 and later became 20 056. It is actually owned by the preservationists of the Caledonian Railway at Brechin in Scotland, where it returned once its hire to RFS was at an end. 2020 began life as D8095 and appears on page 9 in an earlier guise.

David Haydock,
Ricoh Krio,
Tokina 80-200mm zoom,
Agfa CT100i, 1/125 f11.

20 169 was originally destined for the Telecommunications pool when it went into store after a life-time at Toton, but was reinstated in April 1992 to work steel traffic in the Scunthorpe area, being re-allocated to Thornaby. It was placed in store in September 1992 only to be reinstated again in November and taken to Toton. In early 1993, with 20 092, it went to the Railway Technical Centre at Derby for repainting in this livery for the Technical Services Division, which is part of BR's Central Services Division. Duties for this engine, based at Bescot have included Skegness passenger turns and operation on London's Underground hauling civil engineering trains.

Philip Sutton, Nikon F4, 28-85mm AF Nikkor zoom, Fujichrome RDP100, 1/30, f5.6.

In 1993 London Underground Limited joined the list of operators to employ Class 20s on engineering projects. Initially Hunslet-Barclay's 20 906 was sent down to Ruislip Depot for clearance trials and driver familiarization. Hunslet-Barclay subsequently leased two further locomotives, 20 059 and 168 under an agreement with Trainload Freight and BR Technical Services. BRT also provided 20 007 and 092 and the preserved engines D8110 and 20 227 were supplied under an agreement with RFS who were to provide LUL with two machines. This assortment of Class 20s was due to spend three weeks on trial workings on the Metropolitan line track renewal programme, but technical problems saw this reduced to two weekends of operation. This view illustrates D8110, owned by the South Devon Railway, and 20 227, the property of the Class 20 Locomotive Society. The pair are either end of a rake of 'turbot' wagons in Ruislip Depot on 20th March 1993.

Philip Sutton.

British Rail Telecommunications owns twelve Class 20s, which are due to be named after engineers connected with the communications industry. Two of the first four serviceable engines, 20 128 and 131, were sent to Doncaster in September 1993 to be repainted in the new BRT livery. Curiously, only 20 131 received a repaint and the new livery is seen to full effect on the engine as it poses within the confines of the works on 17th September 1993.

Philip Sutton.